AN ALBUM OF
WEST YORKSHIRE P.T.E. BUSES

ROBERT F. MACK

TURNTABLE PUBLICATIONS
SHEFFIELD

Price: **£1.50**

First published 1980

SBN 902844 56 3

Printed in Great Britain
by
Henry Boot Group Printing

INTRODUCTION

The West Yorkshire Passenger Transport Executive was formed on 1 April 1974, its constituents being:

Bradford City Transport

Calderdale Joint Omnibus Committee

Halifax Passenger Transport

Huddersfield Corporation Passenger Transport Department

Leeds City Transport

Wakefield was chosen as the site for the Headquarters of the new organisation, a rather surprising choice as it lay outside the immediate operating area of all the original constituents, but Cleckheaton, which is the approximate geographical centre of the area, was probably considered of too little importance as a town for locating the Head Office there. Each of the four original districts retains its own headquarters and workshop facilities, but the fleet name "Metro" prefixes the name of each of the four districts.

In addition to the original members, the Executive subsequently acquired the businesses of several independent operators: Hansons, of Huddersfield; Baddeley Brothers, of Holmfirth; and United Services, of South Elmsall.

This book provides an illustrated record of the types of vehicle which have been operated throughout the area of the Executive since its inception and, it is hoped, will revive memories of some of the classes which rendered years of service, but are now no longer with us.

Robert F. Mack

1. The Spirit of Metroland. More than a century separates these two splendid examples of British design and craftsmanship as 7061 (RWU 61R), a Leyland "Fleetline", with Roe bodywork, of 1976 vintage, stands in front of the superb Corinthian portico of Huddersfield Railway Station. The whole 416ft facade, with end pavilions, was designed by J. P. Pritchett the elder, of York, and completed in 1847. It is generally held to be the finest classical frontage of any railway station in Britain.

2. Leeds 256 (MBY 347), an AEC "Reliance", with Park Royal bodywork, is seen in the cradle of Middlesbrough Transporter Bridge as it approaches the north bank of the River Tees, while on a private hire excursion in August 1966. New in 1954, it was originally owned by Bourne & Balmer of Croydon, from whom it passed to Holloway (Scunthorpe) in 1965, before being rebodied by Plaxton in 1967.

3. In 1958 Huddersfield took delivery of 188 (NCX 688), an AEC "Regent V", with Roe bodywork. It was transferred from Kirklees to Bradford district in 1974 and is seen that same year passing Norfolk Gardens on the Wrose service.

4. In 1958 Halifax acquired nine Leyland "Worldmasters" with Weymann bodies, along with Glasgow the only British municipality to do so. Originally 372 (KCP 2) in the Halifax fleet, it became 3372, and is seen approaching Halifax Town Hall along Northgate.

5. In 1977, as a result of vehicle shortage, Leeds 284 (5284 NW), a Leyland PD3/5, with Roe bodywork, new in 1959, was transferred to Tyne & Wear, where it was renumbered 415. It operated in the Newcastle area, and is seen here at Station Road, Wallsend, passing Tyne & Wear 604 (SKV 604G), a 1968 Leyland "Atlantean", with Alexander bodywork.

6. Halifax 25 (MJX 25), was a 1960 Leyland PD2/37. It is seen in Commercial Street, Halifax in 1974, before renumbering, but in experimental Metro livery. Note the crest on the nearside pannelling.

7. This 1961 AEC "Regent V" with Metro-Cammell bodywork, was originally 130 (YAK 130) in the Bradford fleet. It was converted to a Metro driving instruction vehicle and renumbered 034. It is seen approaching Ludlam Street garage from Manchester Road in May 1976.

8. About to leave Halifax for Blackshaw Head in 1974 is 3231 (OCP 231), a 1961 Leyland "Leopard", with Weymann body. It was originally Halifax 231 and is operating a former Hebble route.

9. Hebble acquired this AEC "Reliance", with Alexander bodywork, in 1962. It was their No. 664 (PCP 803), and was later operated by Calderdale. In April 1974 it was transferred to Leeds district, and used for carrying staff from Swinegate to Wakefield Headquarters. It was renumbered 23 in 1974, without ever carrying its original allocated fleet number 3023, and is seen in 1975.

10. Halifax 34 (PJX 34) was a 1962 Leyland "Leopard", with Weymann bodywork. It is seen in May 1976, running as Metro Calderdale 3034, in Northgate, Halifax.

11. With "Metro Leeds" insignia over its dark green Leeds livery, 318 (318 DUA), a 1962 Leyland PD3A/2, with Metro-Cammell-Weymann body, passes Eastgate roundabout, while being used for driver training, in February 1978.

12. Smartly repainted in the later Metro Bus livery, 3043 (PJX 43), a 1962 Leyland PD2/37, with Weymann body, enters Barum Top, in Halifax town centre, in June 1979. It was originally Halifax number 43.

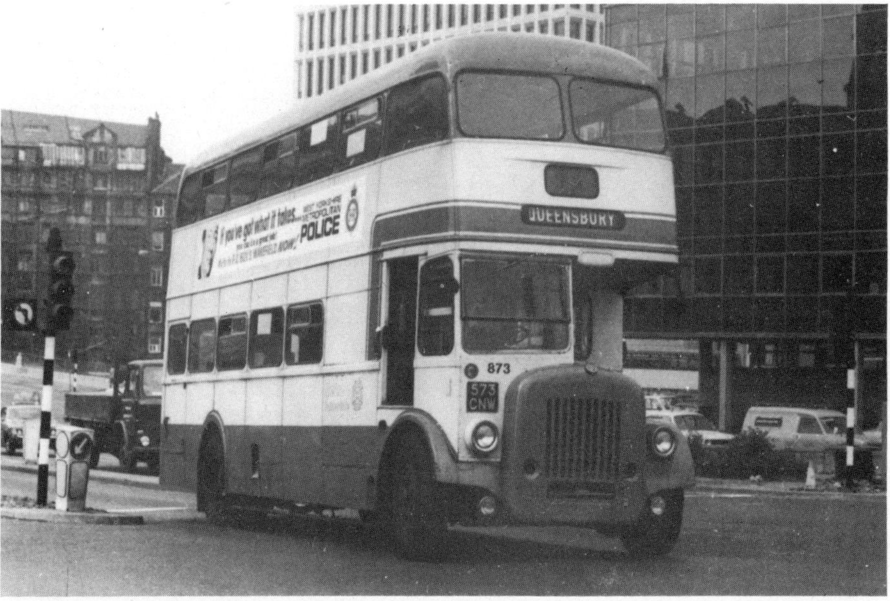

13. Leeds 573 (573 CNW) was a Daimler CVG6LX/30, with Roe forward-entrance body, new in 1962. Renumbered 873 it later passed to Calderdale under whose operation it is seen in 1975 entering Little Horton Lane, Bradford, on its way to Queensbury.

14. Leeds 574 (574 CNW), another member of the same batch of Daimlers as the previous shot, had the unusual distinction of operating for all four Metro areas, and is still used as a mobile publicity unit. It is seen here in High Street, Huddersfield, while serving Metro Kirklees, as number 874.

15. The vehicle in the previous photograph is seen here in March 1978 in its final guise as a West Yorkshire Metropolitan County Council Publicity Unit, at the foot of Easterly Road, Leeds, near the Fforde Grene Hotel. Note the generator trailer on tow.

16. Ex-Todmorden 29 (572 EYG), was a Leyland "Tiger Cub", with East Lancashire bodywork, new in 1963. It became 337 in the PTE fleet, and is seen entering Halifax Bus Station while allocated to Calderdale.

17. Originally 594 (594 FUM) in the Leeds fleet, 894 was a Daimler CRG6LX, with Roe bodywork, new in 1963. It was renumbered following the arrival of "Atlanteans" 556-595, and later transferred to Bradford, where it is seen in Forster Square, still in dark green livery with Leeds City Transport insignia.

18. In 1963 Bradford took delivery of 141 (YKW 141), an AEC "Regent V", with Metro-Cammell bodywork. It became 2141 in the Metro fleet, and was still serving in Bradford in August 1976 when the photographer caught it entering Little Horton Lane on its way to St Enoch's Road Top.

19. Another transfer to Tyne & Wear was Leeds 946 (946 GUA), a 1963 AEC "Regent V", with Roe bodywork. As it stands at Tynemouth, in 1976, the local insignia, superimposed on a yellow background, can clearly be seen; the rest of the body retains its original green livery, though it has been renumbered 411.

20. Bradford 199 (6199 KW) was a 1964 AEC "Regent V", with Metro-Cammell-Weymann bodywork. Renumbered 2199 it remained in Bradford, where it is seen in 1978, but was later sold to Scarlet Band Motor Services, West Cornforth, Durham.

21. Metro 3057 (TCP 57) typifies the style of double-decker so familiar in Calderdale prior to the "Fleetline" era. New in 1963, as Halifax 57, it was a Leyland with Weymann body, and is seen here entering Waterhouse Street, in Halifax Town Centre.

22. In 1964 Huddersfield Corporation took delivery of 108 (BCX 108B), a Daimler CRG6LX, with Roe bodywork. In 1977 it still wore its attractive Huddersfield livery, though renumbered 4108, as seen passing along John William Street.

23. Leeds 104 (104 LNW) was a 1964 Daimler "Fleetline", with Roe bodywork; the split windscreen was a feature of this batch. It is seen in July 1977 on Wykebeck Valley Road, approaching Selby Road.

24. In 1964 Huddersfield acquired 426 (AVN 426B), a Daimler CVG6LX/30, with Roe bodywork. It is seen leaving Huddersfield on the 64 service to Bradford, after it had been repainted in Metro colours.

25. Leeds borrowed several Kirklees-based double-deckers in 1976, including the one seen in the previous photograph. It is seen here at Oakwood, bound for Roundhay Park, on Bank Holiday duties.

26. Ten years after it was delivered new to Huddersfield as 438 (CCX 438B), this Daimler, with East Lancashire bodywork, was still running in its original Huddersfield livery, but carried Metro fleet number 4438. It is seen passing the end of Market Street, near the new Bus Station.

27. Yorkshire Woollen District acquired this Daimler "Fleetline" with Alexander body, as their No. 983 (BHD 222C), later renumbered 132, in 1965. It was transferred to Hebble in 1969 where it became 350, but returned to Yorkshire Woollen District in March 1971, this time as No. 146. In August that year it was sold to Halifax Corporation and renumbered 103. In 1974 it was acquired by the PTE and renumbered yet again, to 3103. It is seen in Bradford in April 1975, still in the Halifax livery it carried till scrapped in 1978.

28. This AEC "Reliance", with Park Royal bodywork, was new to Hebble Motor Services in 1965 as their No. 621 (BJX 134C). It is seen inside Halifax garage, bearing number 320, instead of the 3320 allocated.

29. Frontal contrasts in 1978 at Barum Top, Halifax. Former Halifax 284 (LJX 324C), a 1965 Leyland PD2/37, with Weymann body, is followed by ex-Halifax 95 (JJX 595G), a 1968 Daimler "Fleetline", with Northern Counties bodywork. These two buses were renumbered 3284 and 3095 respectively in the PTE fleet.

30. In 1966 Leeds bought a batch of Leyland "Atlanteans", with Metro-Cammell-Weymann bodies. One of them, 341 (HUA 341D), was loaned to Leeds University for the 1978 Rag Day Procession, after it had been withdrawn from service. It is seen in festive guise at the top of Brudenell Road.

31. Another member of the same batch, 345 (HUA 345D), was transferred to driver-training duties. Renumbered 16, it is seen in 1980 entering City Square, Leeds, from Park Row.

32. A further member of the same batch, 347 (HUA 347D), is seen in Metro livery entering Vicar Lane from New York Road.

33. Our final example of the batch is 351 (HUA 351D), which was transferred from Leeds to Bradford in May 1978. It was out of service from July 1978 to September 1979, then surprisingly returned to Leeds at the end of March 1980. It is seen in April of that year, the sole survivor of the batch, in Woodhouse Lane, near Portland Crescent. It was withdrawn from service shortly afterwards.

34. Entering Bradford Interchange from Bridge Street is ex-Halifax 143 (DJX 143D), a 1966 Leyland "Leopard", with Willowbrook body. It became No. 3268 in the PTE fleet.

35. Another new Halifax bus in 1966 was 101 (ECP 681D), a Daimler "Fleetline", with Northern Counties bodywork, seen entering Orange Street from Great Albion Street, Halifax, in June 1977. It became 3101 in the PTE fleet.

36. In 1967 Bradford Corporation acquired this Leyland PD3A/2, with Neepsend bodywork, which was 242 (FKY 242E) in their fleet. It became Metro 2242, and was sold out of service to Swanbrook, of Cheltenham Spa, in whose smart livery it is seen here.

37. On private hire Metro vehicles occasionally stray into unfamiliar surroundings. This 1967 Daimler "Fleetline", with Metro-Cammell body, was originally Bradford 285 (FKY 285E), and was renumbered 2285 in the Metro fleet. It is standing at Kettlewell, where double-deck buses are a rarity.

38. Huddersfield also purchased Daimler "Fleetlines" in 1967, but their 482 (KVH 482E) came with Roe bodywork. Renumbered 4482, and still operating in Kirklees district, it is seen approaching the Fire Station along Castlegate, Huddersfield.

39. In 1967 Huddersfield Corporation also took delivery of AEC "Swift" 27 (MVH 27F), with Roe bodywork. Still stationed in Kirklees, but renumbered 4027, it is seen leaving the new Huddersfield Bus Station en route for Waterloo.

40. Leeds also purchased AEC "Swifts", with Roe bodywork. Metro 1279 (MUG 479F) was new in 1968 as Leeds No. 79. This view shows it outside the Pavilion, Stanningley, on the now abandoned 405 Shoppers Service, with 1973 Leyland "National" 1301 (SUA 301M) from Calderdale, overtaking.

41. Huddersfield continued to take delivery of Daimler "Fleetlines", with Roe bodywork, into 1968, and one of them, 494 (OCX 494F), is seen in John William Street, Huddersfield, being operated by Kirklees District as Metro 4494.

42. In 1968, Yorkshire Traction acquired several Leyland "Leopards", with Marshall bodywork, including 509 (NHE 9F). This was one of three which were transferred in 1971 to the Halifax fleet, where it became No. 359. It is seen here in 1975, before its final renumbering to 3359.

43. Leeds Corporation bought a batch of Daimler "Fleetlines", with Roe bodywork, in 1967. One of them was 132 (LUA 132F) seen from the Inner Ring Road flyover, entering New York Road from Regent Street.

44. Two of the same batch of Daimler "Fleetlines", with panoramic windows, as the previous photograph, were 142 (LUA 142F) and 141 (LUA 141F). These became Instruction Vehicles 31 and 30 respectively, and are seen on 2 September 1979, at the official opening of the new Dewsbury Bus Station, when they were used as an Exhibitors' Canteen and a Rest Room.

45. Leeds 150 (PUB 150G) was a 1969 Daimler "Fleetline", with Roe bodywork, allocated to Torre Road Garage. It is seen here in its Metro livery, running westbound in Boar Lane, Leeds.

46. Bradford's purchases of Daimler "Fleetlines" in 1968 included 327 (LAK 327G), with Alexander bodywork. It is seen in September 1970 standing at the King's Arms, Greenside, Pudsey, still in its original Bradford livery, and before being renumbered 3327. This service was previously operated by Ledgard.

47. Leeds 363 (PNW 363G), was a 1968 Leyland "Atlantean", with Park Royal bodywork. It was transferred in September 1978 from Leeds to Bradford district, where it operated until June 1979, when it was delicensed. Early in 1980 it entered Kirkstall Road Works, Leeds, later being re-certified and working from Bramley Garage.

48. Later AEC "Swifts" bought by Leeds in 1969, had Park Royal bodywork, like 1025 (SUB 425G), a regular performer on the Hyde Park Circular group of services. It is seen here in May 1980, about to enter Infirmary Street from City Square, Leeds.

49. Still in Bradford livery and carrying its original fleet number, 296 (LAK 296G), Metro 2296, a 1968 Leyland "Atlantean", with Metro-Cammell-Weymann bodywork, passes along Bradford Road, Batley.

50. Another 1968 Leyland "Atlantean" was Leeds 374 (PNW 374G). This one was bodied by Park Royal, and the difference in appearance from the last photograph is quite striking. In this shot the bus is negotiating the large roundabout in Dewsbury Road, Leeds, near the M1 Motorway exit.

51. A later member of the same batch as the previous photograph was Leeds 380 (PNW 380G), seen at Roundhay Park, Leeds. It is passing 1205 (UNW 205H), a 1970 single-deck Daimler "Fleetline", with Park Royal bodywork, serving as a staff rest-bus during a Bank Holiday period.

52. New to Todmorden in 1970, as No. 14 (BWU 690H) in their fleet, this Leyland "Leopard", with Pennine bodywork, was acquired by Halifax in 1971. It was numbered 3330 in the Metro fleet, and is seen in the short-lived single-deck livery, with the two stripes on each side of the indicator box.

53. Bradford only had ten single-deckers, five of which were AEC "Swifts", with Marshall bodywork. One of them, 2504 (NAK 504H), was built in 1969, and is seen standing inside Ludlum Street Garage, Bradford, in 1975.

54. Bradford's other five single-deckers were Leyland "Panthers", with Marshall dual-door bodies. One of them, new in 1969, was 512 (NAK 512H), which was transferred to Calderdale in 1974, as Metro 2512, in which guise it is seen in Commercial Street, Halifax, on West End service. The following year it was sold to Chesterfield Corporation.

55. After moving south, the bus in the previous photograph became Chesterfield No. 12, and is seen in that operator's colours, in the summer of 1976, while on private hire duty.

56. Leeds 200 (UNW 200H) was a 1970 Daimler "Fleetline", with Roe bodywork. It is seen in July 1978 running westbound in Park Lane, Leeds, on the long route from Whinmoor to Calverley.

57. Bradford 413 (PKW 413J) was a 1970 Daimler "Fleetline", with Alexander bodywork. It became Metro Bradford 2413 and is seen entering Great Albion Street, Halifax, at the end of its run from Bradford, via Shelf.

58. Halifax Corporation purchased three Seddons, one of which, 315 (MJX 15J), was new in 1970, and fitted with a Plaxton body. It became Metro 3315, and was transferred to Kirklees with the other two Seddons. It is seen in Metro livery, standing in John William Street, Huddersfield.

59. In 1971 Bradford took delivery of 457 (SKY 457J), a Leyland "Atlantean", with Alexander bodywork. It is seen as Metro 2457 entering the Interchange from Nelson Street.

60. In 1971 Huddersfield acquired 46 (XCX 246J), a Seddon RU, with dual-door body. It was rebuilt by Pennine Coachcraft in 1973 as a single-door design. In 1975 it was still in Huddersfield livery with its original fleet number.

61. An August 1975 scene in City Square, Leeds. A 1971 Mercedes-Benz, with Deansgate Minibus body, 32 (YUA 532J), passes 1968 Leyland "Atlantean" 364 (PNW 364G). In 1979 the Minibus was exported to Malaya, along with four others of the same series. The sixth vehicle, No. 30, went to Sri Lanka during the same year.

62. In 1971 Leeds acquired a batch of AEC "Swifts", with Roe bodywork. One of them was 1053 (AUB 153J), which is seen in November 1976, in an early style of Metro livery, as it passes along Manston Lane, Crossgates, on the long route from Halton to Wortley.

63. A later member of the same batch as the previous photograph was 1064 (AUB 164J). In May 1980 it was still operating in Leeds and is seen on the service to Adel. This was formerly called "Long Causeway", but as there is a road of the same name at the Cross Green end of the service, the name of the service was changed to avoid confusion.

64. In 1977, to honour the Silver Jubilee, Metro 2339 was repainted in silver livery. It was originally Bradford 339 (XAK 339L), a Daimler "Fleetline", with Alexander body. It is seen entering Halifax Bus Station in 1977.

65. Another vehicle chosen in 1977 to carry the special Silver Jubilee livery was the former Leeds 201 (GUM 201L), a 1972 Daimler "Fleetline", with Roe bodywork. It is seen in May 1977 in Boar Lane.

66. In 1973 Leeds acquired 504 (JUG 504L), a Leyland "Atlantean", with Roe bodywork. It is seen entering Princes Avenue from the bus lane at Oakwood, Leeds, on Bank Holiday service.

67. A later member of the same batch as the previous photograph was Leeds 530 (JUG 530L). It is seen in August 1973 on Blackpool Promenade, making its way to a bus rally.

68. Among the last buses to enter service before the PTE was formed was this Daimler "Fleetline", with Roe dual-door body. It was Huddersfield 4144 (GVH 144L), and is seen passing along High Street, near to the Bus Station, still in its smart Huddersfield livery.

69. Another bus acquired just before the PTE came into existence was Leeds 1301 (SUA 301M), a 1973 Leyland "National". Still based on Leeds it was loaned to Calderdale in 1974, and is seen at Rooley Lane on the service from Halifax to Leeds which was then numbered 8, and is now 508.

70. Just before the end of its independent existence Halifax acquired this Leyland "Leopard", with Plaxton bodywork. It became Metro 3009 (UJX 919M), and is seen in April 1975, running westbound in Wellington Street, Leeds, on the through service to Rochdale. This has since been cut back to Halifax.

71. The first vehicle in our collection which joined the Metro fleet when new was 6003 (UWT 603N), a Leyland "Atlantean", with Roe bodywork. It is seen near Catherine Slack, in the wintry conditions of March 1975, climbing towards Queensbury on Service 76 from Halifax to Bradford. It was later transferred to the Leeds area.

72. Early PTE purchases included 8501 (JWU 244N), a Leyland "Leopard", with Plaxton bodywork, built in 1975. It is seen in High Street, Huddersfield.

73. Another 1975 Leyland "Leopard", with Plaxton coach-style body was 64 (GWY 690N). It is seen approaching Manchester Square, on the Central Promenade, at Blackpool, while attending a coach rally.

74. The PTE bought a batch of Bristol LHS6Ls, with Eastern Coach Works Midibus bodies, in 1975. No. 40 (JUG 356N) is seen leaving Leeds City Station approach for the Central Bus Station on Shoppers Service 100. When this service was withdrawn, in 1979, Nos. 38-42 were sold to Tayside Regional Council, whilst 44 and 45 were loaned to Merseyside PTE.

75. The same bus is seen in very different surroundings, as it negotiates a tight bend at Broughton-in-Furness. The occasion was a private hire trip to Ravenglass, for a party visiting the Ravenglass & Eskdale Railway.

76. In 1975 a fleet of Metro Scania double-deckers was acquired. They were all allocated to the Bradford district, and in May 1979 one of them, 2616 (HUA 567N), is seen approaching Halifax Station Bridge, nearing the end of its run from Bradford.

77. Certain routes in the Calderdale area have limited clearance and in 1976 the Executive purchased a batch of ten Low-height Daimler "Fleetlines", with Northern Coachworks bodies. The first of these was 7001 (MNW 1P), seen here in June 1977, as it passes along Great Albion Street, Halifax.

78. In 1977 the Executive purchased a Foden with Northern Counties semi-integral body, for evaluation in the Kirklees area. Numbered 7250 (TUB 250R) it is seen at Embsay Lane End, near Skipton, while taking part in the Huddersfield—Embsay Rally in May of that year.

79. Among the Leyland "Fleetlines", with Roe bodywork acquired in 1977 was 7094 (WUM 94S), which was allocated to Kirklees. It is seen entering Bradford Interchange from Nelson Street, in May 1979.

80. Leyland "Atlanteans", with Roe bodywork, were still being acquired in 1979, and one of them, 6178 (GWR 178T), is seen in Bridge Street, Bradford, in 1980, plastered with advertisements urging support for the local football team.

81. A later member of the same batch as the previous photograph, but allocated to Leeds District, was 6189 (GWR 189T), seen in 1979 in The Headrow, near Vicar Lane.

82. No. 7136 (GWU 136T) was a Leyland "Fleetline" with Roe bodywork, allocated to Kirklees. It is seen in John William Street, Huddersfield, on the Balmoral Avenue service.

83. In March 1980 twenty Leyland "National 2"-type vehicles were delivered to the Executive and allocated to Kirklees and Calderdale districts. They were numbered 1311-1330, and 1329 (LUA 329V), of the latter district, is seen in Great Albion Street, Halifax.

84. Leyland "Atlantean" 6193 (JUM 193V), with Roe bodywork, was a 1980 delivery. The raised driving position can be clearly seen in this shot of it entering Bradford Interchange.

85. Our final offering is 7504 (JUM 504V), one of the five Metro buses delivered for the Leeds District in March 1980. It is seen outside Seacroft Garage prior to entering service on the Easterly Road group of routes.